CONQUERING FEAR WITH FAITH

FROM FEAR
to fear

cecile vasquez

LIFEWISE BOOKS

FROM FEAR TO FEAR
CONQUERING FEAR WITH FAITH
BY CECILE A. VASQUEZ

Published by:

 LIFEWISE BOOKS

PO BOX 1072
Pinehurst, TX 77362
LifeWiseBooks.com

Interior Layout and Design | Yvonne Parks | PearCreative.ca

To contact the author:
www.CecileVasquez.com

ISBN (Print): 978-1-947279-18-6
ISBN (Ebook): 978-1-947279-19-3

DEDICATION

I dedicate this book to Jesus. More than anything, I pray
that all will see you through my story and will come to
know who you really are. I pray they will open their hearts
to you so you can sup with them all their days.

table of contents

acknowledgments

Heavenly Father – I want to take this time to thank you for acknowledging, loving, and believing in me. You have and always will continue to carry me through thick and thin. Thank you for understanding me, making me, and saying I was good.

Mario – Thank you for putting up with my nonsense and silly antics. You are the second closest person in my life next to Jesus because you've always showed me love even when I wouldn't give it back. You always give people the benefit of the doubt, even when you don't have to. You are an example of God's wisdom and patience when I need it the most and a man of integrity. Thank you for supporting me as your wife and encouraging me to pursue and go after what God has ordained me to do here in the earth. I wouldn't do this without God and you by my side.

Mom – Thank you for always making the effort to take time off and go with me to the women's events at church, especially the mother-daughter banquets. I love the little trinkets you bring me because you know it's the little things that matter to me.

Dad – Thank you for helping us when we struggled back in the day just to get food on the table. But most importantly, thank you for raising me and doing the best you could with what you had. Thank you for being a goofball with me in our family because we all need a good laugh.

Helen – Thank you for all the hospitality you show my family. Thank you for coming alongside Dad to help put food on the table and clothes on our backs. and taking care of some bills when times were tough.

Ranella – Thank you, my sister in Christ. Together, we've had our ups and downs, shown our good sides and bad, laughed and cried, prayed and played. I wouldn't trade it for the world, and I'm hoping we keep walking through the valleys and climbing mountains together with Jesus in the center of it all.

Thank you, thank you, thank you to my pastors, friends, and all the people I have met throughout my walk with God for saying a prayer for me, and the ones who have stood in the gap for Mario and me. Without those prayers, I probably wouldn't have made it to where I'm at now, let alone what's ahead of me. Thank you for all the words of encouragement. I pray that it will be poured back out on you, and that whoever prays for us, with all their heart, will receive a hundred-fold blessing in return. I am so very thankful for each prayer.

Thanks to Charity Bradshaw and her LifeWise Books team for helping and believing in people like me to pursue our dreams, all for God's glory.

chapter 1
JUST HEAR ME OUT

Hi, my name is Cecile, and I have a story to tell that I know relates to many out there, both believers in Christ and nonbelievers. I know what you're thinking: what kind of a title is that? I wonder what it's about? "From Fear to Fear"? Just sit down and relax, because I know you didn't pick up this book accidentally. I know you were drawn by the cover and title—you know why? Because God wants to release you from the thing that's been holding you down and has you bound up in your mind. So, listen very closely, because this might sound like your own story, but there's an awesome ending to it.

All my life, I struggled with fear and insecurity, and it wasn't in just one area in my life—it was multiple things that I saw, heard, and experienced down the road as I got older. It was to the point that I was literally consumed with anxiety, having serious anxiety attacks and crazy, dark thoughts. I was fighting for the peace and sanity of my mind—actually, my life. God inspired me to write this book and gave me the name of it as well, because he needs you to see and understand the difference between a good fear and bad one. What I mean by that is, there's the respectable, honoring fear of God that gives you complete peace and joy, and then there's an ugly, gut-wrenching fear that doesn't come from God at all. That fear comes from the real enemy, who cannot be found with the physical eye.[1]

Please believe me when I say this is not a silly, made-up story. This is a true testimony compacted into a book. Understand that I won't be able to share every detail, because this book would probably be the size of an encyclopedia. I know there are tons of testimonial books out there, but I'm hoping and believing God Himself will speak to you through this book. I will say with complete confidence, my book will equip you and bring comfort and healing to you. It will also captivate you with the true, tangible reality that there's a Father in heaven singing songs of love and victory over your life constantly.

I believe the cross of Jesus Christ was a visual demonstration of the Father's love for you. You know that God himself sings a song of victory over you.[2] Yes, it's for God's people Israel, but He's talking to you, too. It's a song of reconciliation mixed with love, and it is just for you. That's what true love is—love will say, "No matter what the cost, no matter how much pain or discomfort it brings my way I will do it."[3] No matter what the world's voice says, a glimpse through the Father's eyes reveals that's how much God loves and desires us. Since the very beginning of time, He. has been so determined to reconcile us and snatch back what belongs to Him. if you have trouble believing it, open your Bible to Genesis 1:27.

Whether or not you are a son or daughter of God right now, get ready because God himself is and will show up and show out personally on your behalf.[4] And I promise, when you choose to stay hungry and expectant for the presence of God, no matter how you feel or what your own mind may think, God will reward you beyond your comprehension so get ready because the change starts now![5]

Endnotes

1. Ephesians 6:12
2. Zephaniah 3:15-17
3. Isaiah 53
4. John 10:16
5. Hebrews 11:6

chapter 2
TRACING BACK

Let's go back a bit and look at my history, starting with the grandparents. My mom was adopted by these people whom I have never met in my life, so I will be sharing with you the things she has told me about her childhood experience. Her father was a shrimper off the gulf coast. I don't know how far they went, but it was said he did make some good money. He also loved to play poker and gamble, and as a matter of fact, he was pretty good at it. He would bring home hundreds of dollars. My mom would get a little something out of it because she had to watch and keep an eye on him when he was in the bars gambling and getting drunk. My mom said he would work for a while and save up his money, then go on one of his drinking binges and do nothing to support his family. I asked my mother if he's an abusive man. She said that she saw and knew nothing of that type of behavior. He was very quiet and kept to himself, not really sharing much with his wife.

Now my grandmother was attending a Catholic church, but some reason she hopped over to a good old Pentecostal church. One day, at the Pentecostal church, everyone was praying all together in another language she could not understand. All of a sudden, she started praying in the same language because God's spirit came upon her, and she fell to the ground! In the church world, that's called getting "slain in the spirit." I laughed because my mom said she was scared when her mother fell on the concrete floor. When my mom told me what happened, I said, "Oh, mom, it was all right—I knew that once she got up from that concrete floor she was going to be as good as new."

As all these things were going on, my mom went up front because she felt a pull to go up there during the altar call. She went up to receive Jesus as her personal Lord and Savior. While at the altar, she started having this hunger for the baptism of the Holy Spirit, thinking about the crazy thing that had happened to my grandmother. My mother said she experienced an overwhelming warm feeling and began crying uncontrollably. But after that amazing experience with Jesus, she started to believe the lying voices in her head saying, "Maybe you didn't receive the baptism of the Holy Spirit, because you're not speaking in tongues." What we need to remember is that when we humble ourselves and come expectant before God, He will give us the desires of our heart. God is the God of all hearts, and it's our faith that activates everything God has promised us. Our relationship is not solely based on works, but believing and receiving what Jesus has done for us on the cross—the action follows because of his goodness. Its grace and faith then that produces active obedience, But I think also it helps to start thanking and praising God and believe that you have already received it and the language will start flowing out.

My mom said that my grandma was a generous giver, and she had witnessed her giving hundreds of dollars to the church. I don't want to be mean or critical, but if my grandmother, whose alcoholic husband worked only part of the year could give like that in those days, why can't the church give like that today? I'm not trying to condemn anybody, but it's the truth. Western culture has an attitude of entitlement, greed, and fear. Sometimes, as in my case, it's a lack of knowledge. I thought we were really giving to God's church but we weren't doing it properly—we were robbing God because we were not giving our tithe (a term for a tenth of our increase or income).[1] I cannot judge anyone's heart, because I made that same mistake for the first couple of years, but I know someone needs to hear this.

Part of the problem is, my mom was never fully active in our lives, and there were times we wouldn't see her for a while. When we moved, my dad didn't tell my mom where we were for an entire year. I believe the purpose was that my dad didn't want us to be exposed to her lifestyle of homosexuality. Eventually, she discovered the place we moved to and would come and park on the outside of our driveway to visit with me for a bit. I can remember her bringing us a little something at times, but it was never brand new. I'm sure there were plenty of times I wanted to go with her, but I didn't think my dad would allow it, and I understand now that he was trying to protect my innocence.

I have only a few memories with my mom, but one thing I do remember was her taking me to the park a couple of miles from my house. I remember someone took a picture of me on a swing, head tilted and with a cheesy smile on my face. I was dressed in white shorts, shoes, and a cute light purple shirt with little white poke dots on it. When we did go visit her, she never stayed in one place; she was always moving from place to place to place, and there was no stability with her. Two things I liked was they would listen to some Spanish music when we they get the cooking, and I also looked forward in seeing her dog buddy, he was known to be a smart dog.

When things got scary back at our house, there were times I thought, "I want to be with my mom." But when we would swing by, she would say we couldn't stay, or she wouldn't answer the door. I would feel let down and rejected because I felt she didn't want us around. The things she told us when we were together about our father were not right, and what is worse, I started believing it. Now that I'm at a mature and understanding age, I understand her behavior; she was smoking crack with her partner and didn't want us around. Her partner was also very manipulating and controlling when it came to us being around my mom. How could we compete with that? It's crazy, because she left an abusive marriage but then jumped right into another bad relationship. I didn't understand the life style my mom was living back then, but I didn't care—I just wanted my mom around.

One time, I was down the road visiting family members and I asked my step mom if I could go visit my mom. She said yes, so I went to visit her. Something happened to make my mom get after me, and I got ticked off at her. I pretty much told her not to tell me what to do because she was never a part of my life. I slammed the door and tried to cool off on the porch. Then she came storming out after me, but I felt she wasn't worthy to discipline me because she was constantly coming in and out of my life, with no stability.

I grew up not trusting her as the years went by because she would say one thing and her actions would go the opposite direction. It's very hard to really trust someone who lies to you. My sisters and I would open up and share with her about the things that were going on in our house, and she and her partner would in turn share their opinions, but they would never actually do anything about it. There were times I really wished my mom could have rescued me from all that crap we had to hear and endure growing up, but there was no real hope of change.

Then there's my father's parents; now his dad was a very hard worker and took care of his family the best he could during those times. If I'm not mistaken, he worked for Alamo, which was a pretty well-known company, and he also did some carpentry work. But his thing was, like some people, he would drink on the weekends. My grandma has mentioned that he would be out drinking during the weekend at bars, and she would be at home with my dad and my aunts. I was told that my grandma would get angry with him because he would come home from the bars drunk and violent, and he was verbally abusive to them. But he didn't have to be drunk to be verbally abusive, and they were all afraid of him. Any little thing could set him off, because it was "his way or the highway," as my dad would say. I remember he was very short tempered, and when we would go to their house to visit, I was afraid because he wouldn't tolerate much. Kids are going to be kids sometimes, but I felt like we couldn't just be kids around him. If we got a little loud or silly, he would come to the living room and start to yell at us, saying he was going to hit us. I don't know how true this is, but my dad has told me before that my grandpa beaten him with the water hose. I could imagine the pain, hate, anger and fear he must have experienced. Hitting someone with a water hose could cause severe burning pain and welts on a person's body.

If you or anyone you know is going through any abuse, run—do not take the abuse, especially if a child is involved. Go get help, let them know what's going on, and separate yourself from that person. Pray for them, and leave them in the Lord's hands. God will answer you. Don't think you did something to deserve it, either. If you made the mistake of getting into a relationship with someone and people were giving you a heads up about them but you didn't listen, don't beat yourself up about it.

I know a lot of people are thinking as they read this, "That's a flat out lie, because I went through similar things. I cried and prayed to God for help but got no answer. Day by day that's all I was experiencing and never saw any change." I know those voices will come, but they are telling you lies. Here's another lying thought: "Just end your life, because nothing good is coming from it; get it over with and just end your pain already." Or, "I'm all alone, and no one understands me." "God's turned his back on you." Those thoughts seem so true and are very tempting to believe. I know, trust me, because I've had those thoughts several times, pounding at my head. But aren't I right? Those thoughts coming at you are ready to take you out from your calling and purpose. (You know you do have a purpose, right?) I will get to the crazy rabbit trails I chased later on, so hang in there, keep on reading, and you will start to understand where I'm coming from.

Before I move on, I would like to say I do love my grandparents. My grandpa is now funny and silly, and way more tolerant than he was in his younger days. I love him, and that's only possible because of the love of Jesus that helps me to forgive him and express it. Now as for my grandma, she was always hard-working and considerate. She was previously a stay-at-home mom and wife to her hubby, taking care of her family. She would wake up very early in the morning before my grandpa got up for work, and I'm pretty sure she got the kids ready for the day as well. She did have her issues concerning my grandpa wanting to go to the bars on the weekends and his abusiveness towards his family.

One story illustrates my grandmother's common sense. My grandpa had come home from the bar drunk; he had a gun and had started threating her. I am not sure how true this story is, but something tells me I don't doubt it. What does a person with common sense do? My grandma locked the doors, thinking of all the possibilities that might happen to them. Then on Christmas Eve, everyone was over at my aunt's house celebrating, as families do, and here comes my grandpa from a round of drinking. My grandma started yelling at him outside and beat him with the broom. I know that was a Christmas I will never forget. It's those things she had to endure because she loved my grandpa regardless of what he did.

Years down the road, as they got older, my grandpa had had a stroke and my grandma did whatever she could to maintain the house, pay the bills, go to work, and take care of my grandpa as best she could. But it started getting to the point to where she couldn't cope with the care of my grandpa. She was getting phone calls at her job from people who had seen grandpa driving in town. She had to get home pretty quick at times because of his stubborn acts; he was just not quite ready to give up yet. Remember, this man had had a stroke, and half of his body was paralyzed from it, but he's bold enough to drive in town. I mentioned he was kind of stubborn, but with all kidding aside, he had to learn to surrender the things we take for granted. My grandparents would argue at times because grandma had to tell him it was too dangerous for him to drive, and she would try to hide the keys from him, so once again, grandpa had to surrender. I've learned, however, being stubborn is actually not a bad thing if it's for pure use—Gods willful purposes for our lives.

I don't think I've mentioned yet that I came from a home of divorced parents, but I was about three years old when that happened. My mom said that it was when my dad beat her up so bad that her ribs were broken and she could hardly walk to the phone to call up her sister and ask her to come pick her up. My mom said in the process of the divorce, she was trying to fight for us, but she said that back then being in the gay life style was not looked on kindly. The judge ruled in my dad's favor for exactly that reason. Right after the judge rendered his verdict that my dad would have the full custody, she went to a little Catholic church and started weeping. As she was telling me this, she began to cry. I think what caused her to be so sensitive is that bringing up her past made her realize she didn't want to relive it again. I do want to know her side of the story so I can be accurate when writing this. What amazed me as she was telling me this is that there was so much I hadn't known. I was told one thing but didn't know what the other side was, so now I know I was upset at the fact I was lied to growing up. But I have to forgive and move on.

Throughout this book, I will mention forgiveness—how to take the most effective steps to begin the process and how to persevere to get free. We have to let go of the past. A saying I've heard many times that is very true points out that unforgiveness is like drinking poison and expecting the other person to die. That's what happens to the ones who choose not to forgive—they're only killing themselves. Now that I think about it, it's like suicide. The best advice is to quit spinning those wheels in your head and forgive already. By no means am I being cold hearted—look at the things I have had to forgive by faith. It's not easy, and our flesh (sinful nature) hates it with a passion, but as the little guy on the Monopoly game says, "the choice is yours," and it is. So, don't be surprised if you're saying to yourself, "Why can't I seem to just break free from this?" It's because you're choosing to hold on to it and not seeking the Father to heal you and to help you get free from it and the person.

Now the process could be an instant healing from your heart, and that's awesome, because it has happened to me before. But normally, it doesn't happen like that, and most of the time it's a process. Numerous reasons exist as to why it's hard to forgive, and every one's different. I will say this from my personal experience: yes, there are difficult things the Lord is helping me to walk out over time, but don't knock the process, because there's nothing compared to having that personal time of healing and deliverance with Jesus.

The process is always here to strengthen you, not hurt you. Our heavenly Father wants to raise up strong and whole soldiers for his kingdom purposes, not spoiled, fussy little brats who want things instantly. What are you going to learn from that? And how are His children supposed to thrive in an evil world when everything has been handed to them? Christians can stand strong amid adversity and not be shaken when we have developed the strength to obey. This is not to say we won't ever feel the presence of evil, but we will still be standing even when the fear arises and not back down; that's courage, not cowardice.

As I said before, we need to forgive, because if not, we are allowing evil to control our life and even the environment. When we are stuck in unforgiveness, we think in some twisted way we're doing justice to the situation, but really, we're keeping ourselves in Satan's prison. It feels right in some sense, but deep down inside, we know it's wrong. Did you know it can open up the door for sickness? No one likes to bring that up, in the church. Why? It points out that we must take full responsibility for our actions and own up to it.

God's not out blaming anyone, ever, and we're not here to do that to ourselves, either, but we do need to take a step back sometimes and reflect. When we discover unforgiveness or other issues, we must own up to it, repent (change our minds), and stay on the course God has us on. Here's an example: before I truly started living for God, I went to go get my yearly check-up and discovered some things that were not right with my body. I had borderline high blood pressure, which I was not happy about because I was thinking about the risk of strokes. So, they told me that they would give me a call to let me know what my results were if something was not right. I

I was nervous for days and sick to my stomach when I got that call. They said Mrs. Vasquez, your thyroid levels are lower than normal, and you need to get on this medicine as soon as possible. I was freaking out, because in my head I was thinking, "What's a thyroid?

Why is it low? Why ASAP? Fast forwarding, I began having severe allergy issues, so I went to a specialist to get further testing. They told me I was allergic to everything outside. I said, "What!" The doctor suggested I get an immunotherapy shot because the allergies were draining and weakening my immune system. That's why I was feeling tired, weak, and had no energy, which was shocking to me because I didn't know allergies could do that to your body.

As I began getting closer to God, He started putting his finger on a place in my heart where I had not forgiven my dad. I called him and said, "Dad, I forgive you." He acted like he didn't do anything, but that's okay, because I did it for me. not him. The next step in the journey occurred when God placed a couple in my family's life to help us with a lot of issues we were going through. I remembered he said to me in sweet, gentle voice, "Cecile, the Lord already healed you when He died on the cross for you. Let's say from now on, by His stripes you are healed."[2] After that, I was on a mission to say that many times a day over myself. At my next doctor's appointment, I was eager to see what was going to come of this. I went back, and sure enough, things started turning around for the good.

So, you see, when I said, "Yes, Lord, I will forgive and take action," everything fell into place. That's why I say, "Don't tell me that unforgiveness has nothing to do with sickness and disease." Once again, I'm here to help by exposing every lie so we can get free. We have to let God deal with the person who has hurt us. If I've learned anything, it's that when we are getting harassed and tormented, it is because of these things. When we're messing around on God by putting people, places, or thing before him; when we're messing around on our spouse, or, dabbling in the occult and choosing not to forgive, we open doors. I'm saying this because I have been in these categories before, and God showed me the truth later down the road. If you're not up for demonic harassment, I suggest you forgive and get your life straight.

I have to believe you're getting the picture now, because I could go on and on with example after example. One of the people I had to forgive was my dad. As I mentioned before, my father endured terrible beatings from his dad and then divorced my mom. He went through a lot of difficult things, including receiving a lot of criticism from his family and from people in the tiny town he lived in who knew his business. Of course, because my mother was gay and left him for another woman, word got around (you know how small towns can be—people tend to know each other's business quickly). Because he was a single dad, I can understand now how difficult it must have been to support three little girls, having to put food on the table and find someone to watch us when he couldn't.

Because my older sister was the most mature, she was the one with the most responsibility for raising us younger ones. I know that could not have been easy, and it prevented her from being the child she needed to be in those years of her life. I don't know if she ever thought this way, but I wonder if she ever wondered "Why me?" "It's not fair," or "I don't want to do this." Right now, I want to speak to the people who have been in this position like my sister: I'm sorry you had to be the one who was chosen to take on the role of a parent; I'm sorry that your life was given to you in pieces. God, I want to say thank you for stepping in to take care of innocent children like us, because it wasn't our fault, either. So, if no one has ever taken the time to say that, receive it, because you deserve it

Look at where I'm at today—God has me writing books and doing other amazing things to take my life experiences and pour myself out, to fill someone up with healing, help, and hope.

Endnotes

1. Malachi 3:8-12
2. Isaiah 53:5 (NHEB)

chapter 3
ALL THINGS NEW, OR MAYBE NOT

A few short years later, we moved to a bigger town in a pretty nice neighborhood that we'd never lived in before. It was all new to me. We had family come over and check it out, and they also lent a helping hand with some projects that needed to be accomplished in due time. They came over for parties as well. It was also nice not having to go to my grandparents' house on the weekends. No offense to Grandma and Grandpa, because I actually would have liked to have switch things up sometimes if it was my choice, but it was refreshing and peaceful being at our house with just the family.

As we moved into our new home, this girl had to start kindergarten. I was not up for it, because I was used to being at home and with my dad. When he dropped me off on the first day of school, I was crying and crying like a baby hanging on to my daddy's pant leg, not wanting to let go. I pleaded, but I had to stay. After a little while, when I had calmed down, I started getting into the groove of things, making friends, napping, and eating snacks. I was a little troublemaker in school because I love to talk and make people laugh, but I also took out my aggression out on a few people who messed with me. Remember, I'm still in elementary school, and I'm acting like a teacher, principal, and superintendent rolled into one. I've been told many times I was born to be a leader, but my little brain was doing its own thing at the time. Thank God, now I'm saved and the Lord is working on my leadership skills, because those ways will not cut it.

Moving forward into my childhood, I began to notice things were getting pretty aggressive around the house. My dad was acting a lot like my grandpa, very mean and abusive verbally and physically. I would get frightened because of the things I saw and heard going on all too often. When I got to the age that I was getting hard spankings, my perspective of him started to change. I had made some friends in the neighborhood, and it was pretty fun playing hide and go seek, blasting music while on the trampoline, and riding our bikes to see who could ride down a steep road with no hands on the handle bars. And guess who mastered that? Yes, yours truly.

I was bold and adventurous as a kid, and truthfully, I want that back. I felt free being on my bike and riding out on the road, letting the breeze hit my face and brush through my hair. One time I was outside playing with my friends in the front yard when my dad began yelling out my name. My friends all looked at me frightened as if they were saying "Good luck," as we parted our ways. I'm not going to lie—as I said, it was frightening, but at the same time embarrassing, too, because I just wanted to play with my friends without someone barking at me.

As I was sharing with a close friend of mine about a few things concerning my childhood, I said, "Now looking back, I felt like fear was my companion my whole life." Let me tell you, there's nothing wrong with having a reliable companion, but when it comes to fear, don't join forces with it. The spirit of fear is so common to the world that it convinces people of things that aren't true and makes them believe things that aren't real. Here's a scripture that coincides with what I'm talking about: "for we are not fighting again flesh and blood enemies, but against evil rulers and authorities of the unseen world, against mighty powers in this dark world, and against evil spirits in the heavenly places."[1] The thing we fight against is the unseen, and it starts with the thoughts that come into our head.

Another frightening moment I recall was when my dad tried to get us to listen. He would pull out this Halloween mask and put it on to scare us, or just for fun he would leave it on the couch head rest. He thought it was so funny, but it was tormenting to me. I often thought with dread within myself, "I hope he doesn't bring that mask out." Parents, I'm going to mention this: please do a self-check to see if you're doing or saying something that could be tormenting your children. Don't brush it off, thinking "I'm not doing anything wrong," and being unwilling to own up to it. If you think it's not harming your child, look at what it did to me. So, start doing and speaking what you expect according to the word of God over your children's lives.

Here's a scripture for you to meditate on for yourself and your children: "Guard your heart above all else, for it determines the course of your life."[2] So in other words, if you hear your children discuss their fears, you may not see the results of fear right away, but watch out, because they could manifest as persistent thoughts or phobias. Be the one to protect and nurture your kids, reading them the word and teaching them the power of confession and taking negative thought s captive. Those are the effective steps for guarding your heart, because if you don't protect it, the enemy will take it through wrong thinking.

My dad had times that he would go out to the bars on the weekends, and my sister would be there taking care of us. I remember one time, right before he left, my dad was sipping on a little liquor and told us this story. I don't know where it came from, but I've heard other people talking about it. He said there were creatures called "la chusas" that were half human and half bird. They had big claws, and they would scratch on the windows at night. I was so scared, and I didn't want to hear anymore, but who was going tell him to be quiet? After he took off, I'm not kidding, my sisters and I put up a thick, heavy blanket on the curtain rod to cover up the windows in the bed room we were sleeping in. You see what we did? We gave in to fear.

Now that I look back on it, I know he told us that story just to keep us in the house. And it worked, because after we demon-proofed the house, we all jumped right in that bed and stayed under those covers. Every time I felt really afraid growing up, I would throw the blankets over my head and stay there, because it made me feel safe and invisible. I've caught myself a time or two wanting to do that in my adult years, but I would hear that sweet, still, small voice say inside of me, "For God has not given us a spirit of fear and timidity but of power love and self-discipline."[3] There are times I have to speak that over myself when I feel fear coming on me, because if I don't speak up and roar the word of God out from my mouth, the devil will start doing the talking, and I won't allow that.

There have been multiple times I've cried out to God and said, "I need your help because I feel I don't want to do this anymore." We're human and God understands when we endure some things for a long period of time, we could get weary. Isaiah 40:31 says, "But they who wait for the Lord shall renew their strength, they shall mount up with wings like eagles; they shall run and not be weary they shall walk and not faint."[4] Here's the thing: we people don't like to wait because we're impatient, and it clearly says those who wait for the Lord shall renew their strength. We don't feel we have time to wait on God when we're in a crisis! I promise you, when you trust God through it all, you will find Christ in your crisis.

For us Christians, that's where the rubber meets the road with our faith. A crisis is to show you what you're made of. Before the crisis comes, we are practicing and studying on the smaller things, like people getting on our nerves at work, but we choose to be patient with them. Or when something unexpectedly breaks down in our house, and there goes the little savings we had left. We may want to curse out of anger, but we say, "No, I'm staying in the peace of God." I believe the devil wants to see if we truly believe the word. There's knowing the word, and then there's a whole other level when we believe the word even if all hell breaks loose. It will break you or break you up. I'm expecting every crisis to make me, and make me more like Christ.

Endnotes

1. Ephesians 6:12 (NLT)
2. Proverbs 4:23 (NLT)
3. 2 Timothy 1:7 (NLT)
4. Isaiah 40:31 (ESV)

chapter 4

CURIOSITY WILL KILL THE CAT

The first time I was introduced to a ouija board, I was around the age of ten, completely unaware of what I was getting into. My uncle had put it in the back of the shed. I heard they had been trying to get rid of it and couldn't and there were demonic events happening in their home. So me, my sisters, and my cousins all surrounded the thing. I was both skeptical and curious, because when others had tried it before me, I said to myself that they had to be moving it. When I put my finger on it, my cousin started asking it questions, and it started moving. I was shocked it was moving so smoothly. I asked her, "Did you move it?" She said, "No!" I'm thinking, "This is nuts—how can it do that? All of a sudden, my uncle came and asked loudly, "What are y'all doin'?" We all got scared and jumped. My heart was pounding, because he scared us coming in like that and thinking it's funny—but it wasn't. I should have known, because of the stories I've heard, and the way it was hidden in the shed. I knew I should have left it alone.

I know now for a fact that we opened up a whole can of worms to the dark side. After that, my sisters and I would draw out that board on paper, find a nickel or something, put our finger on it, and start asking it questions. My sisters have told me one time that they both on different occasions saw a black figure in the shape of a man. One sister said the figure was talking to her, but it didn't scare her. When I would take a shower and close my eyes to

wash my hair, I would see scary characters from movies I'd seen. I would instantly open my eyes so those thoughts would leave my head, and I would hurriedly dry off, get my stuff, bolt straight to my room, and close the door. I hated the dark and the night time. I know some of you are thinking, "Those characters are fake—it's not real." I agree, but that's what the devil used to torment my mind, and I gave in because I didn't know any better at the time.

It was catching up to me, because I never wanted to go to the bathroom at night since it was pitch dark in our house at night, and my dad would turn off every light. I would hold it as best as I could till the morning, but sometimes it didn't work. I would have an accident on myself and try to cover my tracks, because I could have gotten a spanking for doing that. He probably was thinking, "Is this girl ever going to learn how to go to the bathroom? I would get spanked for this, and he never bothered to ask me what was really going on.

Parents, I want to say this, don't assume you know why your kids are doing the crazy things they're doing. Stop the assumptions, sit down one on one with them, and get to the root of it. Find out why they keep doing it. And if your child doesn't want to talk about it, then go straight to God with the problem. If you want to intervene in your child's life, do it with prayer first, and not automatically the way you think it should be done. I'm talking about praying over your children everyday what the word of God says about them, as a child of God, and affirming their destiny. You will always need to pray for your children, so don't give up until you see what you've been believing for come to pass.

One day I was thinking about intercession when a thought came to mind that made me curious: it was the word "intervene." I decided to google it, and lo and behold, it said "intercede."[1] That's what we as God's people do when we pray—we're pretty much "butting in," but doing it the right way—God's way. In our flesh, we want to butt in the wrong way with our own opinion, and it ruins everything. We need to stop it, and do it God's way. Here's a scripture for us as parents and for our children: "And if you leave God's paths and go astray, you will hear a voice behind you say, 'No, this is the way; walk here."[2] We can get off track, too, so that's why I say this is a scripture for all of us. We need to be praying over ourselves, because we could veer off the Lord's path.

Don't give up on your kids—you could be the only one who's consistently praying for them daily. They're your babies, your flesh and blood, and you have what it takes because you have God Himself living on the inside of you. Your children are our future Moseses, Deboras, Marys, Anas, Davids, etc. They're paving the way for the coming of Jesus. God needs them, whether you or anyone else believes it or not. How do you expect God's will to be carried out until the coming of Christ? I don't understand why some preachers say, "God doesn't need us, and He doesn't need anything from us." Are you kidding me? How are things supposed to get accomplished on the earth if He doesn't have His people in agreement to do it?

So, surround yourself with a church body that not only has the ability to help you but the will to do it. Find people you know will be there for you, backing you up with love, prayer, encouragement, and truthful accountability. Pray and ask him what church to go to if you're not going to one. Tell him in your own mind, and ask Him to confirm it if you're not one hundred percent sure. Also pray that God will connect you with the right people. That's what I pray, especially if He's sending us to a new church family. Now, when I was in my younger years in school, it would bother me because there were a few girls who would look at me funny and even ask silly questions about my body. I wanted to respond in anger, but I didn't because I wasn't going to go there.

One girl I particularly had issues with rode the bus home with me. This girl would tease me pretty much every day, no joke. I would dread going on that stupid bus because she would always come near me and call me names. On and on, day after day, this girl continued, but the funny thing was, this girl was a scrawny, loud mouthed child. You would think since I was bigger than her I could have beaten her in a fight, and you're right. That's how Satan is—he comes off as big and scary, like he's got power and authority over us, but he really doesn't. See, all he has to do is speak to you and intimidate you with his words, and if he succeeds, he's got you trapped and paralyzed, just like I was with that girl. In reality, I could have put her in her place, just like I do to Satan now. Stand up for yourself, and don't let that stinky devil make himself out to be someone he's really not to you.

Endnotes

1. "Intervene". *Dictionary.com*. Web. 16 August 2017. http://www. dictionary.com/browse/intervene?s=t.

2. Isaiah 30: 21 (TLB)

chapter 5

AS SHE THINKS, SO SHE WILL BE

When I was told by many voices that I was fat and ugly so many times, I took on that identity, but Jesus opened up my eyes through the scripture. Song of Solomon 6:5 says, "Turn your eyes away from me, they overpower me. Your hair falls in waves, like a flock of goats winding down the slopes of Gilead." He loves my hair—it's very pretty to Him. I can believe that, because he did create me, and everything God himself created he declares to be good. Eyes say a lot—they are the window to your soul.

Every year up to the fifth grade, I would always get sent off to summer school—it never failed. Maybe it's because that's what I was expecting. Remember, what you expect without a doubt you will receive in full, so be careful what you're expecting, because it could become your reality. Every time the teacher would ask me a question, more than likely I wouldn't get it right. It was embarrassing, because everyone stared at me, waiting to see what my answer was going to be. I wasn't as good with math, and I hated it too. It was like a whole other language to me. It involved a lot of thinking, and my little brain at the time couldn't take it. I've missed out on some chances to win awesome prizes, but my belief that I was stupid, especially with math, meant that I got nothing.

Every Friday, I had another chance to be left out. On Friday, the school had a library-style cart full of different snacks to sell. Pretty much all the students in my class got something, because they had money. But me and this other Mexican girl didn't have any money to purchase anything. We would look around at everyone else and stare at each other with sad looks on our faces, saying, "I wish I could have got something." Honestly, if I had had money to buy both me and her something I would have, because I wouldn't want her to feel left out.

The good news is, when Jesus died on that cross for your sins, He did it for everybody, not just a certain class, race, sex, etc. He included everybody, because he doesn't like anyone to be left out. During His days here on earth, he was despised and rejected so many times. I could totally relate to that; all of us can, one way or another.

Of course, not all my childhood was terrible—I do remember when my dad would take us to Six Flags every year, and that was pretty fun. Another awesome memory I had was watching Disney movies, because I had a ridiculous collection, I love those movie, mainly the classics. The recent ones are sometimes pretty cool, but others I question because they have too much witchcraft, and I'm not defiling my conscience over modern Disney movies. So, have fun with your kids—play outside with them; buy some kids' paint and paper and let them be creative; go to the park and play ball, or whatever—life's too short to sit around and do nothing with these little gifts God has given you. This is what I say—simple, but profound in its way—it's better to have fun with little than have everything with no fun at all. Your children want your full focus, time, and love, no matter what they do wrong.

In middle school, I was more curious then I'd ever been before, and that's when puberty springs forth. I liked it in some ways, because the environment was different—not like what I was used to, but do-able. I had no problem making friends, because of course, Cecile was the class clown/chatter box. I loved to fool around in class because it made my day go by faster. In one of my classes, there was a boy who was quite large—bigger than me, I know that for sure. He had the nerve to punch me on the arm and thought it was funny. He didn't know who he was messing with, because if he had known the environment I lived in at home, he would have known I would not put up with getting hit. Out of reaction rather than response (I believe those are two different things), anger got hold of me, and I stabbed him on the head with my house key. He was furious with what I had done to him. He told the teacher, who called security, and they escorted me out of there faster than I could say "hallelujah," because I didn't want to be there anyway.

The assistant principle began asking me why I had done that, and he told me even if I was defending myself, I still shouldn't have done that. Then he said he was going to have to call my parents. I thought,

"That is not a good idea. Does he know how my dad handles things around the house?" I never grew up in a Bible-believing Christian home and didn't even know God, but I was praying and begging God in my head, "Please, Lord, don't let them answer that phone." As he called my house for the hundredth time, I was thinking of all the possibilities that could go wrong, but finally he got it in his head to stop calling.

I was slowly but surely learning my lesson about how to stay in peace and not sin with my anger. I could have really hurt that boy, but the good news is his big head was fine—there was no puncture wound, and I think he and everyone else knew it. I knew I was wrong for my actions, even if I had been trying to defend myself. I should have told the teacher and not taken matters into my own hands. It was a valuable lesson.

Endnotes

1.   Genesis 50:20

chapter 6
RISKY STUFF

During those first years of puberty, I became aware that guys outside of my school were taking notice of me. These were people I had met at parties or a relative's house. These thoughts would constantly roll through my mind: "Don't have sex because you can get pregnant or catch something nasty." I was afraid--in my mind, I really didn't want to, but my heart wanted to be loved by a guy, so it was a battle. I eventually hooked up on and off for a couple of years with a guy I really fell in love with, but his behavior toward me was monstrous. The reason I say this is because we had a long-distance relationship, and he would take advantage of it by staying out all night doing nonsense. He would yell at me when I asked him what he was doing, or why he didn't answer my calls. I would hear about the crazy things he was doing from others. It's not that I'm putting him down or want to label him, but he was the bad boy type of guy. For some strange reason, that's the type of guy I would usually attract.

Our relationship was dysfunctional, but I've prayed several times for him and his family now that I'm in my right state of mind (the mind of Christ). I'm believing him and his whole family will come to Christ and live for him all the days of their lives. I don't hate him at all, and when the Lord brings him to my mind, I pray.

When I was writing this book, opening up, and sharing my personal stuff, I felt a little fear, wondering what people were going to think. But it was mixed with condemnation at the same time, because of my sexual promiscuity. Then the scripture Isaiah 54:4 came up: "Fear not; you will no longer live in shame. Don't be afraid; there is no more disgrace for you. You will remember no long the shame of your youth and the sorrows of your widowhood." I've heard Joyce Meyer as well stand on that scripture, because it's powerful and liberating to our soul. We don't have to carry around that suitcase of guilt, shame, condemnation, and regret. Just choose to drop that off at the cross, because Jesus knows exactly where it goes. He's here to take the luggage that you were not meant to carry, and I promise He will get rid of it for you. I'm writing this with complete honesty and transparency, because Jesus and I are here as a team together to free you with my story. I have nothing to be ashamed about because Jesus took my shame.

I want you to read the story of Joseph in the Bible, in Genesis 37-47. It may be kind of lengthy, but what God did in his life is so powerful. Here is what Joseph said to his brothers that did him wrong: "You intended to harm me, but God intended it all for good. He brought me to this position so I could save the lives of many people."[1] That makes me want to write, because that's exactly what God is doing right now to those who are reading this book right now. He's turned my mess into his beautiful message of grace, and that's His plan for you, too.

I wasn't perfect growing up—I would lie about things I was planning to do behind my parents' back. I would tell my dad I was going to hang out at a friend's house, which I did, but if he had known what was going on over there, he wouldn't even let me set foot in that house. So, after some convincing, he would let me go, and that house would sometimes end up like Cheech and Chong. I heard her mom say one time, "if I caught you smoking cigarettes, I'm going to beat you." But she would allow them to smoke weed. I wondered at first if I was hearing it right, because I couldn't believe my own ears. I'm thinking, "Wouldn't you want it the other way around?" I dared not say anything to her, because she would probably put me in my place.

The silly thing was, I myself was smoking with them, getting high, and eating anything in sight before crashing. I really thought that it was the fun, cool thing to do because it made me relaxed. I was not much of a drinker and didn't care for it at all. My friend's sister was a pretty girl, but she had dark circles around her eyes and heavy bags that aged her. I don't know if it was from all the smoking she did or not. I was grateful that my dad never found out, because he would have forbidden me to go to her house anymore, and he would have dealt with me as he saw fit.

Sometimes we mask our pain and sorrow with things like drugs, alcohol, sex, shopping, or gaming. As human beings, we are meant to take it to Jesus when we're feeling like we want to run to a piece of cake. Then when we're done getting our fill of whatever it is, we're even more down in the dumps than we were before, and it was all self-medicating. I know, because I've run to the joint, I've run to the fridge, I've run to the stores, and many other things. These things that our sinful nature runs to can't do us a lick of good, so we need to put those things down and run to Jesus for help.

I don't ever want to share stores about my past and not lift up Jesus, because I'm not here to boast of worldly things, but only Jesus Christ and what He did for me. Another story of God's grace and protection on my life, involved the same friend as before, but a different location, as they had moved into town. My friend had a party, and her dad was there, but not her mom. The house was filled with friends, loud music, and tons of weed all out on the table, so people began to smoke. I'm not sure specifically how it all happened, but the cops came knocking on the door. Me, my friend and her dad ran like little roaches to her parents' bedroom and acted like we had been asleep when all this was going on. I was freaking out and saying to myself, "I'm going to jail, we all going to jail." We waited a short while with hearts pounding, because we were waiting for something to break out or maybe a raid. It got quiet, and none of us wanted to get up, but one of us managed to do it, and everything was okay. I'm thinking, "Thank you, God, none of us got in trouble," because all I had been thinking before was "slammer time."

God Himself was very merciful, not only to me but to all of us, because our lives could have been ruined from one stupid party, but

He didn't allow it. In Jeremiah 31:3-4, it says "The Lord appeared to us in the past, saying; I have loved you with an everlasting love; I have drawn you with unfailing kindness. I will build you up again, and you, virgin Israel, will be rebuilt. Again, you will take your timbrels and go out to dance with the joyful." God, the whole time, was drawing me with his loving kindness. He knows the plans he has for me, and he was going to rebuild my life like never before. I didn't realize at the time God was giving me so many chances, but I was too caught up in that life style.

As time went on, I met up with this other girl who was kind of quiet and kept to herself, but I managed to pursue her and make conversation. Time passed, and she invited me to stay the night at her house, so once again I convinced my dad and he approved it. He was expecting me to be back by the next morning, sharp. We hung out, enjoyed making ice cream malts, and watched a little TV. Then she asked if I wanted to go chill in her room, and I said okay. To my surprise, she introduced tarots cards to me. They looked pretty cool, with intriguing pictures on the cards. She began teaching me step by step how to use them and so forth.

Silly me, I didn't know what these things were since I'd never seen them in my life. I thought this was all innocent, because it looked like a card game. But that's how crafty Satan is—he's a snake slithering in the grass, and we need to be a people who see him from miles away and crush his head! I opened the door for demonic disaster in my life because it created a huge open door for destruction years down the road. Parents, monitor what your children bring in and out of the home, and also who you let your kids hang around with. Be on guard, because if you're not, the enemy of your soul will be more than glad to take charge. I was getting sucked into the enemy's lies.

It felt a little weird at first, reading people's cards, but then It started becoming a high. I felt like I had a power and knowledge that no one else could know. When I thought I was helping people out, the devil was pulling the wool over their eyes as well. Further down the line, I started reading books on witchcraft and astrology, and then turned to occult movies and games like Harry Potter. I would hang around at times with a lady who was doing the same things as I was, but probably had been at it longer. These people are not always obvious; they dress just like us. Don't let TV and movies fool you, making you think that they're always dressed in black, flying on brooms.

I also had a ring from the medieval days, which had an opening on the top to hide poison in, so the wearer could secretly poison an enemy's drink. Did I use it for that? No, but I thought it was cool to wear. Did I ever have thoughts about using it on someone? Yes, when they kept messing with me. One day I was in my room reading a book with spells in it, and I had the bright idea to do a spell on my dad to shut him up and have peace and quiet. I'd had about enough of him yelling and hitting me when he got into his really bad moods, and I saw this as a way out. I was not trying to harm my dad, as in killing him, but I thought this was going to be the way out of my misery. It was not right what I did at all, and he still wouldn't even know it to this day unless he were to read my book.

I know one thing, the Lord showed me I needed to release him from that and repent, breaking that spell off him, and that's exactly what I did. I didn't want that to be a hold on his life anymore. I love my dad, and even though he did what he did, I want him to know that. But as I performed the spell, I noticed it was kind of working. The reason I say that is because it was quieter than it's ever been. But did you see what I said, I said that it kind of worked, because it lasted for maybe a couple of days, and then it was like Bengay—it wore off. But unfortunately, the devil increased my faith for the dark side, and it didn't even work one hundred percent. Anything Satan does with one hundred percent excellence is like the Bible says: it's only to steal, kill, and destroy.[1]

> *"For you are the children of your father the devil, and you love to do the evil things he does. He was a murderer from the beginning. He has always hated the truth, because there is no truth in him. When he lies, it is consistent with his character; for he is a liar and the father of lies."* [2]

When I read this scripture, I thought, "Ouch!" because of the truth that was presented without sugar coating. When people don't live for God, they're pretty much doing the work of Satan himself. Jesus doesn't say these things to be harsh with us, or because He wants to call us names, but He needs people to see they're either with Him or against Him. So, let me ask you, what are you allowing the Father of lies to do through you? Same-sex relationships, fornicating, gambling, pornography, adultery? I'm here to help you, not shame you. The greater thing is, Jesus already knows. He just wants you to give it to him. He's done with seeing you hurt, confused or angry. He wants to make you new on the inside so you can shake the world around you on the outside.

Endnotes

1. I John10:10
2. John 8:44

chapter 7
THE BURDEN OF MEMORIES

I was sitting down one day, just talking to God like I normally do, and I began thinking back on my child hood days. I have mentioned before that concerning my own life, God has blessed me with a pretty sharp discernment. I think Satan observes what gift God has put on the inside of us and comes up with a plot to use it for his own devices. I can feel or sometimes see the spirit that people carry. It's not like I'm trying to see through the person, or look for something bad, but it's something I just know. God's not out to shame a person and label them evil—that's the thoughts of Satan.

For example, one day, when I came home from school, I turned the corner into the kitchen and saw a woman with my dad. I'm just being honest, but the thought that came into my mind was "witch." I know that was Satan's voice, but I felt something was not right. Little did I know, this lady was to become our step mother, and God bless us both because we didn't get along. I'm not out to shame and sabotage people; I'm here to lead people to Jesus Christ, because it's about Him, not them. I was a Daddy's girl and very close to him, so I didn't want anyone to take that from me.

As the lady became part of the family, my dad and I grew apart from one another. I used to sleep in my dad's room because I felt safe with him, and that's what we did back then. She stopped that because I was getting to the point that I needed to be in my own room already. There were times I would cry for hours on the floor in front of his bedroom door because I wanted to be with him, and I wanted her to leave. I was so mad at her one time that I told her I hated her, and sad to say, at the time I really did felt that towards her. I felt like some of the things she did were out of spite towards me, but now I know it was Satan working through her.

One of many embarrassing moments in my life was when she would take us outside and check our heads for bugs and my friends riding their bikes were all looking my way. One day, my little sister and I were there at the house by ourselves, and I said, "Let me clean your head for bugs." I got the towel and wrapped it around her neck, got the roach spray and the chino (lice comb), and went to town on her head with the spray. My parents walked in and were furious, and I got hit by my dad. I was crying and felt hurt because if he only knew, my step mother had done that very same thing.

It frightened me when my sisters got hit, because the screaming and yelling was like someone being tortured. I'm not exaggerating when

I say that, and I'm not trying to make him out as some beast, but if you were there, you would understand. At times when my dad was hitting us, and it was way out of control, my stepmother would step in and put a stop to it. I felt she should have done that in the very beginning. Once again, these were the thoughts that rolled around in my head. That's why my heart was so hard towards her, because of things like that.

I saw that almost everywhere I went, the devil was attacking me through someone to bring me down. When I'm going through any kind of attack, I like to speak this scripture out loud to myself:

"though a mighty army surrounds me, my heart will not be afraid. Even if I am attacked, I will remain confident. The one thing I ask the Lord the thing I seek most is to live in the house of the Lord all the days of my life, delighting in the Lords perfections and meditating in his temple." [1]

I would keep this scripture handy so when things went down, I would already have this in my heart so I could fight the devil with it and see him scatter. I wish I had known this scripture earlier, because now it's a part of my arsenal. Plenty of times I've been lying on the floor of my bedroom floor sobbing my eyes out, wishing to have a new family. I remember being in my room with a knife slowly going back and forth on my wrist, wanting to die. But I stopped, because fear overcame me, and I couldn't proceed with it. The surprising thing was, everyone was in the house but no one walked in on me. I was to the point that I wanted someone to, for attention.

If you could take a picture of my heart, it would look like suicide, because that's what my life looked like. I wanted the pain to stop;

I just wanted it to go away already. I felt like I was just a waste of space, a person with no value. I just wanted someone to believe in me and see that I was worth something. I remember a song with the following lyrics: "Oh God can you hear me, Oh God are you listening, Am I more than flesh and bone, am I really something beautiful? Because I want to believe, help me to see."[2] I don't care if you are a guy or a girl—that's the heart cry of every human being. We yearn in the depths of our being to be wanted, loved, and affirmed without judgment. God Himself is the perfect candidate and only one who can and will do that. The Father wants his daughters to know "Yes, I love you," "You're beautiful," "You're smart," "You have a purpose." To His sons, He's saying, "I'm proud to call you my son," "You're accepted," "You can do anything," and "I'm here for you."

You have to accept that, because it's the truth. Believe it for yourself, because no one can do it for you. It does take spending quite a bit of time with God, reading/studying the Bible, praying, and speaking the word of God over yourself. After you do all of that, start living like God's children. And I promise you, when you are determined to stay consistent in your relationship with God, things will start to turn around for you good.

Endnotes

1.   Psalm 27:3-4
2.   Mikeschair, "Someone Worth Dying For," *A Beautiful Life*, Curb Records, 2011.

chapter 8
ENOUGH IS ENOUGH

Another time in my life, my sister and I got in trouble for something I honestly don't remember. My dad called us to come outside. We were scared by the tone of his voice. I was the first one to step into the garage, where he was waiting. All of a sudden, out of nowhere, I got hit with a board straight across my legs. I had serious burning pain on my legs. I was screaming and crying, touching the back of my legs where I felt two puffy welts. They hurt so badly, it was painful to walk sometimes. When my sister came out, he did the same thing to her, and the board broke.

I couldn't get excited when summer came around, because my dad would sometimes go beyond making us help do the yard work. He would make us get down on our knees pulling out weeds all along the fence, and it wasn't a small one, either. He even had me pulling weeds from the rose bush, even if it meant my being there in the dark while he sat back, relaxing and drinking a cold one. I dreaded him cutting the grass, because he would have us rake it up, put it in clean trash cans, and drag the cans to a pasture behind us to dump it. We did this over and over, hours' worth of work, when it was hot as heck outside with tons of blood-sucking mosquitos. I would cry out of frustration because I was being eaten by mosquitos, trying to hurry up and get the job done. To this day, I hate mosquitos with a passion.

We managed to stick it out and get through it. I'm not going to lie—it still feels a little uncomfortable writing this because it's my past. I find myself wondering how he could be so cruel to us. When you have your down moments, or you're going through something really tough, I want you to do yourself a favor and read this scripture: "For I know the plans I have for you, says the Lord. They are plans for good and not for evil , to give you a future and a hope. In those days when you pray I will listen. If you look for me whole heartedly you will find me." That gives me hope, because He wants us to have a future. He's not hostile to me or you, because His thoughts/plans towards us are good and not evil. We just need to get into alignment with him.

I'm so done with the devil himself speaking through the mouths of people and telling us that God's mad at us, He wants nothing to do with us, and He's disgusted with us. That's all a lie. I'm tired of people saying you can't do this or that, you need to look a certain way, or you need to buy something. I'm not here to be like someone else—only Jesus, because He is an awesome person when you get to know Him. He saved me from death and hell; He healed me; He showers his love on me all the time; He helps me when no one can; and He doesn't judge or criticize me. Today, right now, can be your day. All you have to do is simply call on Jesus and say, "I need you—I can't do it anymore. He will show up, I promise.

Other things that have happened to me have happened to thousands every day. I have had a few relatives step out of bounds and try something. I knew it wasn't right, and most times I broke away, but there were a few situations I got entangled in. I know some people don't like to talk about this, but I have to. What we keep inside could eat us alive. In other words, telling these stories is not so much about exposing a person but a demon. When we open up our mouths and release what was on the inside of us, the enemy loses ground in our lives. When I learned to talk about sexual abuse with my husband, because I trust him, I felt freedom. The darkness died on the inside of me, and life came back into me. I dare not let the enemy label me, nor the people who did these things, because God loves us both. I have nothing against them, and I love them.

Fast forwarding again, I was in a relationship with someone at school, and everything was okay, but once again, I was the one who had to take charge. I showed him I wouldn't put up with any nonsense and would tell it like it is. Two years later, we broke it off because he was cheating on me. As it turned out, that was one of the best things that happened in my life, as you will see later.

After that happened, I changed schools because I moved in with my sister. I hated that school because some of the students seemed stuck-up to me, and I was used to people at the other school. A few months later, I dropped out because I had no use for that school and definitely didn't want to go home, because I wanted to do life my way. And all I was looking forward to was partying, drugs, sex, dating, and tarot card readings. I was the life of the party—loud, rude, and obnoxious, but I wasn't happy—I was actually really miserable.

My mother and I grew close during that time because she also lived with my sister, and we would share the same room, but we also partied together. I would be partying with friends all night, literally. I also saw relatives flirting with each other, and two girls in a same-sex relationship wandering off together. We were all messed up, and I would think at times, "This is crazy, what am I doing here?" But I chose to stay because I loved to party—that was my life.

The truth is, God put destiny in me before I was in my mother's womb; He knew down the road I was going to turn away from this immoral, filthy life style and live the life of faith. Take a look at this scripture:

> *"By faith Moses, when he became of age, refused to be called the son of pharaoh's daughter, choosing rather to suffer affliction with the people of God than to enjoy the passing pleasures of sin, esteeming the reproach of Christ greater riches than the treasures in Egypt; for he looked to the reward. By faith he forsook Egypt, not fearing the wrath of the king: for he endured as seeking him who is invisible."*[2]

It's an honor to serve the one and living God. He could have cast me out and completely cut me off from his presence, but He didn't want that, because that was never his plan to begin with. To me, it's worth living this life because I know I have help, strength, and anything I need from God. He delivers all that, but it's the relationship I'm most grateful for. He can't wait to hear my voice say, "Hello, Jesus" every morning. Why wouldn't I? I mean, He gave me the breath to give it back to him in my worship. He yearns for our affection and attention, and He would not force it.

Endnotes

1. Jeremiah 29:11-13
2. Hebrews 11:24-27

chapter 9
MY BLESSING IN DISGUISE

So, I was at my lady friend's house relaxing and cooking with her, me and another lady friend got to talking. One of them mentioned the name Mario and asked if I was interested in him. I said "Ew! Gross! Heck no!" He was not my type, and I couldn't see myself with him at all. I couldn't seem to go there. I'd seen him at parties, but never had any kind of interest in him, mostly because of a few things that turned me off which I will not mention. My friend's relative had to go to the store, and I went with him—lo and behold, who came out of that store? The guy we were just talking about. I said, "This cannot be a coincidence, could it?" All the sudden, this joy overcame me. I got out of the car, gave him a hug, and asked how he was doing? Then we swapped numbers.

He got in his car and took off, and I stayed in the car, waiting for the guy I came with. He came out the store looking angry. He began cussing at me and wanting to know why I was talking to the other guy. We both had been involved, but we were only using each other to get the little things we wanted out of one another. He was reacting out of jealousy and didn't like it one bit that I was reaching out to some other guy. I didn't care, because this man meant nothing to me, and I did whatever I wanted to.

A little time went by, and I began to wonder if I should call the other guy. I was kind of afraid, but I decided to do it. He answered, and we started to talk—or maybe I did most of the talking, because he was kind of quiet or shy. For every question I had, he gave me an answer. I asked him, who are you related to? How many siblings do you have? What's your favorite color? Your favorite number? What kind of food you like? It was so elementary, but I didn't care, because it was pure, simple, and innocent, and I felt like I could be myself around him. He pulls that out of me, and it's a good thing, because I don't have to perform and be someone I'm not.

He's a very laid-back kind of guy, but also with a little adventurousness in him, which is a good balance. Night after night, we would talk on the phone really late, with my eyes closing and the phone coming loose in my hand, but I didn't care. Mario would come down on the weekends with his brother when they had days off. I would come and visit, and we would chat for a while. Our conversations were good, and he was definitely attractive to me, but I didn't have feelings for him in the way I needed to.

One day, I said to God, "You need to do something, because I'm not feeling it. Let me know if He's the one, because I'm not wasting my time." One hot and muggy night, we were sitting out there on the porch talking again, and he was being Mr. Cool. He said, "When you kiss me, you will see sparks." I started laughing to brush it off, but when we did, God did something, because I never felt the same towards him. So, we began to grow closer and closer to one another, with him coming down to visit and more long chats on the phone. I said, "Okay, are we officially dating? Are we now boyfriend and girlfriend?" We came into agreement and said yes.

Not long after that, we moved in together, and things were pretty good. He got a job because I told him I wasn't going to be with a man who didn't want to work. That's the same as being abusive or a cheater. I had my own job, but things started to get rough after that. We fought almost every day. He was easily influenced by certain family and close friends, and that is where a lot of the arguments came from. He would defend them and not me, which would fuel my fire, because I believed if he loved me, he should defend me. I would be working late hours at my job and come home sick to my stomach with fear that he wasn't going to be home.

When I came home, sure enough, he wasn't there because he was out and about drinking, doing drugs, and going to certain places he shouldn't be. Or I would come home and find him drunk, lying on the bed with the beer bottle tightly in his hand. We broke up once or twice, and it affected me a lot because I really loved him. I knew he was a good guy, and he was not like the men I've been with before, despite his addictions. Don't get me wrong—I would do drugs too, but I started slowing down to the point of quitting because of my job. I did drink a little, smoked cigarettes, and partied.

It wasn't easy, because he had a lot of people who would want him to do what they wanted for their own selfish reasons. He wasn't seeing that, but I was. I would say something to them, because it wasn't right, and I know that's why they tried to get in between us, but that's okay. We're still here, together till death do us part. Satan wants you to think that one puff won't hurt; one sip won't get you drunk; if you have one affair no one would know; and one dollar in the slot machine won't make you broke. He's a liar! Jesus said in John 10:10, "The thief comes only to steal and kill and destroy; I have come that they may have life, and have it to the full."

The thief that was described is Satan and his demons. That's all they think, live, and breathe, twenty-four hours a day. The one who said, "I come to give you life to the full," that is Jesus himself; that's all He lives, thinks, and breathes, is life, because He is the way, the truth, and the life. We as human beings think we're so smart, but guess what? We're not, because if we were, we would be healthy, rich, and truly satisfied with our life everyday all by ourselves, which is impossible. I need God's love, forgiveness, peace, salvation, and more because I'm tired of living for myself. It's a miserable life, thinking and being like that.

Mario and I would fight like cats and dogs: "Why did you take long at the store? Why are you looking over there? What were you doing?" I was always in constant fear and jealousy. Those times that we split up, I blamed myself for it, because I was becoming an uncontrollable monster who drove him away for the reasons I just mentioned. One night, we were in the apartment, and I was fixing to jump in the shower. I felt in my gut not to do that just yet. When I came out, he started getting into "fiend" mode. He said,

"I'm going go to a friend's house really quick." I said, "Why?" He said he was going to buy cocaine from a friend who sold it to him.

I stood by the door and said, "You're not leaving." He said he was never raised to hit a woman, so I should move out of the way. I asked him not to go. He was trying to move my body over so he could leave, but I stood my ground even more firmly, determined he was not going to leave me. I started crying, slid down to the floor and was begging him not to leave. I told him he only thought these people were his friends, but if they were, they wouldn't be taking his money and killing him at the same time. He said, "Cecile." I was still bawling my eyes out, and he said my name again, trying to get my attention. And when I lifted my head and opened my eyes, something happened, I couldn't explain it, but I know that I know something happened because his face was different. He embraced me, and I felt a peace, so secure. Before, he had been either drunk or on something, which is how I know something happened to him. He looked sober, as if he had never been under the influence of anything.

The next day came, and everything was good—he didn't seem to want drugs. The next day passed, and he was still good. Then days passed, and I knew he was completely delivered by the power of God. See, I didn't know what it was or what to call it, but that's what happened Mario told me when I made that comment about his friends taking his money and killing him at the same time, something hit him. But it was ultimately Mario's choice to say in his heart that he would stay. I truly believe that was an action of his faith, and he obeyed in not going. That's how God came in with his mighty power and delivered him. To this day, he does not crave or desire anything like that, because of the keeping, delivering power of God.

This stuff is real and amazing, but you have to obey the one who truly cares about you who's here to help you. The Lord started sending people to our apartment who invited us to go to church. We were never rude to them, but on the other hand, I never took it as a big sign from the Lord. But when we moved into a house, Mario knew the landlords, who were old church members. Then another person started coming by who turned out to be his old pastor, from the church he grew up in. We still went about our life and moved on. A couple of times in the middle of the night, Mario would wake up holding his throat and gasping for air. I was having sleep issues that kept me up all night, so thank God when I saw that. I was able to step in to try and help him by blowing air in his mouth, almost like CPR. Then he caught his breath and was back to normal. We knew that something was not right, but we were lazy and never bothered to go get it checked out.

So, when we moved into that little house I mentioned, it popped up again. One late afternoon, I was cooking, and I got this phone call from a girl. She said, "Are you Mario's wife? Wondering who this could possibly be, I said, "Yes, why?" She said there was no need to worry because Mario was okay, but she needed me to come down there. I was trying so hard not to panic, I almost bolted out the door and left the gas stove on because I was cooking our supper. When I got there, I saw police cars and the ambulance, and Mario was farther away in what looked like a crushed Coke can. Before I could run out there to check on him, I heard people say that they might have to fly him to San Antonio because it looked bad. I yelled out, "Mario are you okay?" He lifted his arm up and said "Yeah." I said, "Oh, thank God." I knew that he was confirming what I felt, when I was rushing to get there, but an unexplainable peace came to let me know that he was okay.

I followed him in the ambulance and finally had the chance to ask him face to face what happened. He said he was driving home and dozed off with the cruise control on. He heard a loud noise from the road because he was driving on the rumble strips, so he woke up, drifted to the other lane, and over-corrected. When he did that, the Explorer flipped over a couple of times and landed on its tires, but it was crushed on both sides. A few people from both our families came to the ER, and before I went in to talk to him, they began saying he must have broken or punctured something in his body for the car to have looked that bad. They were going on and on, saying negative things, but something in me wouldn't allow me to believe that nonsense. I said, "No, he's going to come walking out just fine.

It was hard to explain, but I just knew everything was okay. They checked him and did tests because the wreck was so terrible, but after they did all those things, they said everything was fine, nothing broken or damaged. The only injury was a large purple bruise from the jarring of the seat belt and soreness. But he walked out of there because of the divine protection from God Almighty himself. One thing Mario told me is that when the car was flipping, he yelled out, "Jesus!" That's the power and authority that's in that name, I still haven't heard of anyone saying Allah's name or Buddha's and getting saved like that. Consider that before you think about using that name in vain.

When you call out the name of Jesus with all your heart, believing he will answer you, amazing things happen. My husband wouldn't be here with me today if it wasn't for him calling out that name and the Lord responding back to him with His protection. Remember when I said I felt I should take him to the doctor but never did?

That feeling was God telling me to take him. When I didn't obey God and put things off, I opened the door to Satan, who has tried to kill Mario I don't know how many times in his life. Each time, it seemed like it would be a sudden, quick death, but by the grace of God he did not allow it to happen. God has an amazing plan for his life. Hopefully, one day you will be able to hear the testimonies concerning his multiple death experiences and how God preserved his life.

After that accident, we felt led to go to the sleep center place because I had a feeling it was sleep apnea. They did the overnight tests, and sure enough, he had it badly, to the point that he was losing around half of his oxygen, and it was slowing down the brain function. That's why he was waking up in the middle of the night holding his throat and gasping for air, because his throat was closing on him. He would easily fall asleep within minutes on the couch at church and be knocked out quickly at bed time. Please listen to me: when the Lord tells you to do something and you know it's Him, just do it, because it can save you so much pain, heartache, and trauma. If you're seeing symptoms in someone such as restlessness, fatigue, falling asleep quickly, insomnia, or choking during sleep, please get help, because it could save that person's life. If you can't afford it, try to find help—pray and ask God for direction. Do what's needed to get them help.

Endnotes

1.   2 Corinthians 10:4

chapter 10
HEADED TO THE CROSS

Despite all these things going on, we very slowly started going to the little Baptist church Mario grew up in. Little did we know, even through there were a few things we disagreed with, seeds were being planted in our hearts. After that, God led us to another church, which was where we really needed to go for who God was calling us to be. It took Mario weeks to adjust to that new church, because it was the polar opposite of what he was used to growing up, which to me felt very uptight and conservative. But I just knew when I walked out of that church it was the one, because the same peace I felt in that car when Mario had that wreck showed up in my heart.

So in the next service or two, I gave my life to Christ. What I'm about to say is not intended to discourage you, but after I gave my life to Christ and began taking those first little steps to live it out, all hell broke loose. I know you're probably wondering how that could be. Shouldn't it have been better? Giving my life to Christ was the best decision I could have made; He knew I was going to need him more than ever for what I was about to go through.

When I became a follower of Christ, I learned a lot in a short time. I never understood how I was able to learn so quickly, but I did. I learned and witnessed the power of confession, healing, the power of the Holy Spirit, and other things. Sometimes I didn't even know what I was saying, because it didn't make sense to me. But then there were things I knew and understood, and I began exercising my faith. Some days were rough, and then I had my wonderful new believer moments where every time I opened the Bible to read, it's like the words were jumping out of the pages at me, ready to come in and be hidden in my heart. God would give me signs, and everything was great because He was making Himself real to me.

I didn't grow up in a home that faithfully went to church to serve, study the Bible, and so forth. Every time a negative, fearful thought would enter my mind I had to learn to say, "No!" and speak the scriptures from the Bible that pertained to the attack against me. I was so tired of the devil getting into my head and attacking my thoughts. He has no right to tell you what to do. He cannot control your mind, although that's what he wants people to think. He wants you to believe he has full control, and you can't do anything about it at all. I'm going to say this: we can't completely put a stop to ever having negative thoughts, but when we identify one, we do not have to keep it there. It's a fight, but the only way we can have victory in overwhelming thoughts is with the word of God.

We have to be vocal and aggressive with the enemy. He might tell us we're crazy and stupid for doing that, but it's the truth. Here's a scripture to prove it:

> *"We use Gods mighty weapons, not worldly weapons, to knock down the strongholds of human reasoning and to destroy false arguments. We destroy every proud obstacle that keeps people from knowing God. We capture their rebellious thoughts and teach them to obey Christ."*[1]

So, it's one thing to replace a bad thought with a great thought from the Bible and dwell on it, but there are going to be times that the only way to stop bombarding thoughts is to speak the word of God, aggressively and out loud. Once you speak something out your mouth, your mind has to stop focusing on what you're saying. Keep speaking the word until you have the peace of God. Pray out loud Psalm 23 over yourself, even if you have to do it over and over. Do what you know to do.

That's why it's so important to not only read, but study the Bible and get it into your heart so you can recall it when things come against you. A solider always stays fit and prepared before he goes out to battle. Does the military take a new person, slap a uniform on them and immediately give them a weapon? Certainly not! Do we seriously think this person would be able to protect anyone without any tests, training, or equipment? No way—we would probably all be dead, because they hadn't been trained and equipped properly. They need to prove themselves worthy as a true soldier. I also believe they need to be completely sold out in their minds about laying their lives down for us all. Thank God for our military.

I am so thankful for the Holy Spirit. A few years into my born-again walk with God, the Holy Spirit used a trustworthy man of God that he had placed in our lives pointed out something to Mario and me. This was somethings I'd never mentioned to him that I still had in my house. Even though I was a born-again Christian, loved Jesus with all my heart, and was a new creature in Christ Jesus, I still had things in my home that were connected to the old life I use to live. I had Harry Potter games, witchcraft books, rated R movies, and if I'm not mistaken, tarot cards as well. That's the light being shined on darkness, which was still inhabiting my house. To be honest, it had never dawned on me at all to get rid of those things.

After we left the house, I told Mario we were not going to bed at all until we stripped the entire house of darkness. We were up pretty late, but I didn't care, because my soul and future with Christ was way more important to me than my sleep that night. Mario gathered all those witchcraft demonic resources, put them straight into the trash barrels, made a fire, and burned it all up. The funny thing was, we were in a burn ban and didn't even know it. The tiny town we lived in had cops driving around throughout the day and into the night. But I believe God covered us that night because he wanted the darkness to leave our house.

We need more men and women of God in the church who are Holy Spirit led and bold enough to bring up things that need to be talked about rather than shoved under the rug. In Hosea 4:6, it says, " My people are destroyed from lack of knowledge. Because you have rejected knowledge, I also reject you as priests. Because you have ignored the law of God, I also will ignore your children." Ouch! But it is true that when God's people choose not to get in the Bible so more of His word can abide in them, they are setting themselves up for disaster. They are leaving themselves wide open for demons to operate and make their lives miserable. Remember, their only mission in life is to kill, steal, and destroy. It's not that Gods wants to ignore his people, but how can he help us and show us our blind spots when we are not giving him our time and attention?

That's one of the tricks the enemy uses; he wants you to believe spending your quiet time with God first, before anyone or anything else, is nothing but a waste of our time.

Let me tell you something that is a fact in my life: when I spend time with God in the morning and am patient with him (because He's certainly patient with me), He begins to show me His heart and His ways. He has shown me how and what to pray, because He knew the weapons the enemy had set up for me that day. I've had multiple visions of my real home in heaven, and I saw our son that I had miscarried up there with Jesus, with his other brothers and sisters in heaven. I could go on and on; I've had prophetic words given to me about my husband and other things. I'm hoping you're really starting to get how super-important it is to give the Lord the first of your day.

There's one thing I want you to think about today: what's in your home that could be attracting and attaching itself to you so it can attack you? I'm not being mean—I said it before, and I'm going to say it again. I'm here to help you, not harm you. It's about purging—God's cleaning up and perfecting not only you but the things around you, because He knows the things around you affect you and can pull you, either towards good or evil. The flesh hates this process and doesn't want anything to do with it, because it's an enemy towards God. But it's okay, because you have God's spirit inside you, and He's always there to help you conquer that sinful nature that's at war with God in you.

Take a good inventory of your house, then ask Holy Spirit to show you the things that need to be removed at once and move on, never looking back. Get rid of the things He wants you to remove from your house now. Then replace them with God things. For example, any demonic books you throw out should be replaced with good Christian books that will feed your mind good things. Movies that are no good, full of foul language, nudity, and magic should be replaced with Godly movies. Any pictures or posters on your wall that idolize the things of the world and are not lifting up Jesus in your life—get them out of there. That's why I told you to pray, because the Holy Spirit will show you what you need to do, not me. He's the boss. I trust whatever He tells you, and you should be obedient to what he tells you, because it's for your good. No one likes to be purged, but it will produce great things.

Here's an amazing fact: eagles are created for high altitude, but snakes are not. It is said that when an eagle takes the snake up in the air with him, the snake's oxygen level starts to decrease. It pretty much chokes the life out of the snake, because it's not meant to be in high places like that. That's the devil—when you dwell in the most high (God's presence), you're an eagle, in a high position that cannot be touched. The enemy gets choked out by the presence of God, because He can't handle God.

He hates God and anyone that is of God, and He knows He's been defeated by God through the blood of his son Jesus Christ. He was the seed of the women that crushed the head of the serpent, which is Satan himself. Here's a scripture about the eagle in the Bible, which represents us: " But those who trust in the Lord will find new strength. They will soar high on wings like eagles. They will run and not grow weary. They will walk and not faint."[2] When you put your complete trust in God, you will find new strength. That means I will find a new type of strength I've never had before, because it's a new level He's bringing me into. I believe when you have new strength, that means a new level of glory, a new level of wisdom, new understanding, brand new joy, etc. It's like God giving us a brand-new pair of shoes we've never had in our closet before, or a new shirt, something that's never been used. But I truly believe when Mario and I took that step of faith in burning all those Satanic resources, we were renouncing Satan and the covenant I made with him years back when I messed with that Ouija board.

Endnotes

1. Isaiah 40:31

chapter 11
HELL ON EARTH

From there on out, it was literally a fight for our lives. What I'm about to tell you is something I really had to pray into, because this is serious stuff. For that reason, especially in the church, people often don't want to open up and talk about it to someone. I know for certain this is all for God to be glorified, and to show people that it wasn't by anything I did because it wasn't humanly possible for me and Mario to come out of it alive. I believe it really started after I burned up the dark stuff up in my house.

One day, out of nowhere, darkness really started pounding on the doors of my mind day and night. And this was not just for a few weeks or even months—it was longer than that. I felt a Satanic, consistent oppression against my mind, which is something I have never experienced in my life. It was so bad that I would never wish this kind of attack on my worst enemy. I started getting anxiety attacks multiple times a day. The enemy would put a thought in my mind and as a baby Christian, I didn't know warfare. I would just sit down and cry. Yes, I would call out for God to help, but I didn't know how to stand on the truth of his word because I didn't truly believe his word. The enemy tricked me through my lack of knowledge and my negligence in studying the Bible.

My life really started to spiral down from there. I think the first lie I believed was "you're alone," and then it became "What if you're alone and your dying, or something bad happens to you and no one is there to help you?" One thing after another, like sharp fiery, invisible arrows came right at my head, nonstop. I was doing my ultimate best to speak out the scripture, pray around my house, and attend church and small group. But it just seemed like it wasn't enough at the time, and I didn't understand it, because I was getting beat up constantly by the devil.

Then the thought would pop into my mind that the word has no power because I was still in this mess. I was still having anxiety attacks, and I felt I was never going to get out of it. Once again, I was fighting this thing with all my might, but I was starting to come into agreement with these thoughts because I was still in the same position, and nothing had really changed at all. In fact, it had gotten worse. This is what I learned: " we walk my faith not by sight"[1] as the Bible says. That means we walk or live our life out of who and what we believe, which is Jesus and the Bible, not by what our physical senses see, hear, feel, taste, or touch. Now I'm not telling you to play dumb and deny those things God has given you as a gift to help you in your daily life, but I'm saying when darkness comes against you, do not trust or depend on your senses.

We need to trust in the words that are in the Bible above all else. When you hear the word, faith automatically comes inside you and makes the faith you have now stronger to the point you are totally convinced. That's what my problem was. It's not that it wasn't working; I just needed to keep listening to it to the point that I was totally convinced, and that takes time and patience. So faith comes from hearing and hearing through the word of Christ.[2] We have to keep hearing and hearing continually. You can speak it out of your own mouth, buy some Christian resources, or find a pod cast and listen to it in the mornings when getting ready, on lunch break, and before bed. And of course, read your Bible to yourself. There are many easy, quick, and affordable ways of hearing the word so it can have a powerful effect on your spirit and every area of your life.

So I would stare at the bottle of thyroid meds I had, thinking Lord, I'm too young to be sick. God completely healed me from that, and hopefully that will be in my next book. The thought popped into my head, "You're going to overdose on those pills and die. I was scared—I didn't even want to get near that bottle or look at it. I began crying and saying, "No, I'm not." Then the devil knew that didn't work out in his favor. He would go to something else, like strawberries, for instance. I stopped eating them because I was afraid my throat would close up on me and I would die of suffocation due to an allergy. Do you see what he was doing to me? He was putting me right in his corner of torment.

I can't even tell you how paranoid I was about so many things. I had no rest in my mind or my body. I couldn't even go as far as hearing something negative on the news, because I would go into a panic attack. I decided not to watch it anymore. I couldn't even have anyone over to my house to visit me, because thoughts would run through my mind that it would be really embarrassing if they saw me having an anxiety attack right in front of them.

Let me help you to expose the enemy: he would personalize the thoughts, as if I were talking to myself. He wants you to think it's all coming from you. Not to say we don't ask ourselves questions or think about something, because we do. But let me ask you this: who in their right mind would think sick, twisted, paranoid thoughts for the fun of it? He wants you to believe those are your thoughts, when in reality, those are his, to kill, steal and destroy. When a thought pops into your mind think ahead: is this thought here to kill, steal, and destroy my life?

With finances, when you know you want to do the right thing, here come these opposing thoughts tempting you to spend your money; or you know you love your spouse, but like every other marriage, you're not perfect and you get in a huge fight—here comes that thought, "She/he was really not the one you were supposed to be with." Or for me, I was doing well in exercising and eating better than I have before, and here came that voice: "I want a big fat, juicy burger," because I haven't had one in a while, and I have been doing really well. So why do I need to treat myself with food that's no good for me when that's exactly what God's helping us to overcome so we can be strong in our latter days, to do his work and to enjoy our lives?

The enemy either personalizes thoughts to make it seem like they're yours, or he comes straight to the sinful nature and smooth talks so you go after what you want, rather than what God wants.

Remember, Satan is a master deceiver, which is why we need a true relationship with Christ, not just a religion. It's a person, not an organization. If you think about it, it would be pretty messed up if God, out of all the things he created, cherished a cat, a dog, or the sky more than me, and that's because I'm made in his likeness. How do you think He would feel if God saw you cherishing and worshipping an organization and not Him? Or another person like the Virgin Mary, and not Him? Not to knock the mother of Christ, but she didn't create me, God Almighty did. He said, "Let's make man/women in our image," so that we would look like Him. I believe the way we look like God is by his spirit that's in us.

So, with one thing after another, the enemy was trying to bring me down fast and hard. I was so hopeless I wanted to die, or at least for everything to stop, because I just couldn't seem to truly enjoy my life.

Endnotes

1. 2 Corinthians 5:7
2. Romans 10:17 (ESV)

chapter 12
AT THE END OF MY ROPE

I was depressed, oppressed, and just tired of fighting for the peace and sanity of my mind. I'd heard stories in church of certain women who were put in a mental hospital because Satan had done to them what he was trying to do to me. It frightened me, because the thought was running through my mind, "That's what he's trying to do to me." But the good news was, people close to those ladies were praying faithfully for them. God came through and healed their minds, and now they're living and doing the things God has assigned for them to do. Everything in me was ready to shut down and give up, because it felt like too much for me to handle, but God wouldn't let me. He would stir up the fighter in me, and I would keep on keeping on.

Just a reminder for some of you: God told me, "It's my word that defeats the enemy, not yours." I know what he meant by that. You know how we can get so mad and frustrated at the enemy that we start saying things like, "You're an idiot," or "I hate you." That's not going to drive him away, but rather closer to you, because you're talking the way he does, and he wants you to stoop to his level. So, don't go there just because he wants you to.

I want to share a significate dream concerning warfare. I will tell you what it means, because I want you to know how important your dreams are, Gods speaks to you through them, but once again the copycat Satan does, too. I had a dream that I was in a little run-down home, and at the front glass door, I saw a black Tahoe pull up. Immediately, I knew it was evil, and I said, "Shut the door." The door was closed, and I ended up in an empty room and with a demon-possessed boy a couple of feet away from me. We were standing in a warrior pose, ready to battle it out with one another. The spirit opened its mouth, and no sound came out, but a red orb did. It came toward me, but not at a fast pace, so then I opened my mouth, and a white orb went straight to that demon. Then something interesting happened: the white orb that came out of my mouth devoured the red orb that came out of that demon's mouth. So, when I was sharing this with a lady who helped counsel me, she began laughing and said, "Wow, it was the word of God that defeated the enemy." The word carries its own weight with power and authority.

One more interesting thing pertains to what happened before I went to bed and had this dream. I know this may seem a little too personal for some, but I'm sharing this so you will know how demons operate. My husband and I were spending intimate time together, and I couldn't focus because all of a sudden, I felt depression trying to come over me. I didn't want to say anything, but when it was time to go to bed and Mario went to sleep, I saw in the corner of my bedroom a little demon-possessed boy standing there looking right at me. Then I put two and two together and realized this was the spirit I had been feeling, and now I got to see it with my own two eyes in the spirit.

I texted my friend and told her what I saw, and I told her I knew I was not dreaming. As I tried to comprehend what was staring right back at me, I heard the Holy Spirit with stern authority command that spirit of depression to go, and that's exactly what I told it to do. I commanded it to leave my bedroom in Jesus' name, and it left. But that spirit was the same one that showed up in my dream trying to torment me. I know you're thinking, "What!" Yes, the spirit world is alive and well, more than you may know it to be.

I can't tell you all the demonic attacks I was getting in my sleep when I gave my life to Christ. Don't freak out, because my journey is not your journey, so don't assume what happened to me might happen to you. One time, I felt like I was being lifted off my bed, with the covers being pulled off me. Was it just a dream or did it really happen? I still don't know to this day, and don't care. One time in a dream, I felt something covering my mouth, but I couldn't see what it was. I literally couldn't say the name of Jesus, because it was trying to stop me. They know they have to flee when the name of Jesus is spoken. So, I said, "Okay, I will say his name out loud in my mind." Sure enough, that demon had to take his filthy hand off my mouth.

But through it all, the Lord was teaching me about warfare and His word. He was making me stronger through it all, because trials can motivate growth. I truly believe that, because one of the first things we ask is whether we have done something wrong, and if so, what is it, so we can correct it? When bad things happen, don't always think it's your fault, or God's up there in heaven with a sledge hammer teaching you a lesson. But those difficult things make us open up our eyes and soften our hearts to see the truth about lies we may have believed for the longest time. I know that's what it was for me, and I'm glad that through God's lovingkindness, He showed me some things that were not right with my attitude, or a twisted belief that wasn't from God, or that my actions were only producing selfishness and pride on my end.

I also believe God wants us to grow from other people's mistakes so we won't have to go through heartache and loss. We are also to obey what we read in the Bible as well. So, like I said, I learned how to fight demons, and things started to ease up for me. My mind started to ease up as well. But here was the problem: the enemy let up for a little time, but he wound up coming right back even harder. And without my seeing it, he would knock me down again, leaving me feeling like I was back to square one. It would really discourage me, because when I thought everything was cool, here he came and blindsided me out of nowhere.

This is why I declare this scripture over myself, so it can strengthen my spirit, and remind me that Satan hates me because I come from God, and he wants to take me out any way he can. 1 Peter 5:8 says, "Stay alert! Watch out for your great enemy, the devil. He prowls around like a roaring lion, looking for someone to devour." I really wish I had taken this verse super-seriously and made it part of my arsenal back then, because maybe I wouldn't have taken off the armor of God and been naked in the spirit when I began to relax. I don't have time to go into a lesson on the full armor of God, but it's so important to go back and read it. Do some research on the armor, which is discussed in Ephesians 6:10-18, because I want you to learn how to study and research it for yourself without being spoon-fed.

chapter 13

THE THOUGHTS SATAN HAD FOR ME

Now one night, my husband and I were lying down to get some sleep, so he was already dozing off. He never has a problem dozing off quickly, but I, on the other hand, began to experience tormenting thoughts stirring up anxiety. When I said earlier in the book that I had to fight for our lives, this is what I am about to tell you. As he was asleep and I was fighting off those thoughts, the darkest thing I have ever experienced in my life began oppressing me, and I know only the grace and love of God got me through this. Thoughts slammed into my mind about killing my husband with a huge knife in our kitchen. I would go to prison, my life thrown away, and I would be tormented in a prison cell because of murder. I was seeing these demonic visions like a story, one clip after another, going through my head nonstop. It scared me, and I started crying because those thoughts were getting out of control.

I was trying to stop the thoughts, but they were too overwhelming, so I woke up my husband. I was crying and crying, saying, "This is not me; I don't want to do that," and Mario was asking me, "What's going on?" I seriously didn't want to tell him, because thoughts in my head were telling me not to say anything to him, because he would think I was a psycho. He kept asking me over and over what was wrong, and I wanted to tell him so badly, but fear had me by the throat, threatening me. Finally, I told him everything. That demon didn't want me to expose the plans he was cramming into my head.

That's the first step you can take in rendering a demon powerless--expose him. Go to a Christian, or someone you know without a doubt can help pray and agree with you. If you don't know a true Christian to open up to, I would stop the mind games with the devil and call out the name of Jesus right then and there. Don't try to fight it on your own, because you will not make it, period.

At the end of this book are two different prayers you can pray. One is to help you invite Jesus into your heart and life so he can help you defeat your giant. The other is a deliverance prayer to help you renounce and break off some things attached to you like a leech. I'm right here with you. and so is Jesus. I feel him right now saying, "I'm right here. You're not alone. It's okay—you don't have to fight this alone anymore." Open your mouth and confess those dark thoughts you're having. Expose the voices in your head that are evil and telling you to do things that are bad. You need to tell someone, whether it's a Christian or Jesus himself, because He's waiting, and I'm telling you, your healing starts there.

"Therefore, confess your sins to each other and pray for each other so that you may be healed. The prayer of a righteous person is powerful and effective"[1] Pray with someone, or use those prayers in the back of this book. The enemy wants you to hide those thoughts and voices in your head, but I would confuse him by prayer and thanking God for all the good things He's given you and what has taken place when you called on His name.

When I confessed to Mario, I told him to put away the knives. I was crying in terror because I told him I didn't want to hurt him. What he said next at first sounded stupid, but it was actually a wise thing that had to have come from God at that very moment. He said, "No, I'm not going to put up those knives, because that would give Satan more ground in your life." At that moment, I wanted to smack him and say, "Are you stupid? Did you just hear what I said? Later, though, I really started to understand, and maybe someone needs to hear this. Whatever those thoughts are trying to get you to do, don't do it. I know you're probably thinking, "But it's hard," and I get that. But you're operating in faith every time you tell the enemy no and resist his instructions, and God's got your back, because he only responds to faith.

Remember that even though Gods' got you covered, the enemy will try to convince you otherwise. Of course, we know in reality it's a lie. I like this acronym for fear: False Evidence Appearing Real. Remember that every time the devil tries to lie to you about something. He is the master distractor, deceiver, and destroyer of your destiny so you won't be effective to destroy his kingdom of darkness and help bring forth the people to the light (Jesus). That's why I always turn to prayer and the Bible. God will always show me the truth of who He really is, but also be my helper and give me direction.

It was tough for me and Mario, because Satan wanted me to kill myself and my husband. I fought with everything I had, and I felt like I was hanging on by a thread, but God got me through it every time. Whenever I felt that heavy oppression come over me and it got too overwhelming, I cried out to Jesus to please help me. I know you're probably wondering why God allowed me to go through something so dark. One reason is to free you and inform you, so you can be the key for someone God puts on your path to help open their prison door.

I've heard this saying in the church a lot: "hurting people hurt people," and it's so true, but the Holy Spirit told me one day, "Free people free people." I'm sorry, but I've never heard that one in the church world. Nonetheless, it's so true, and I believe that's a word of conformation for you saying your freedom is near—it's closer than you know. That's God's desire and will for your life, to be completely free from worry, fear, and anxiety.

Endnotes

1. James 5:16 (NIV)

chapter 14
GETTING TO THE ROOT OF THINGS

I want to share another revelatory nugget the Holy Spirit dropped in my mind when getting out of the car at the grocery store: "Your problem is not anxiety, you doubt me." I was surprised, because anxiety was what I was focused on, but I realized it was true when I was thought about it. I asked Holy Spirit to show me what the root of all this was. It had to do with abandonment and rejection, being out of control, and things either taken from me or not given to me as a child. It stems from my childhood, because I've always felt like I was left out and not wanted. Throughout my life, things were taken from me or denied me when I needed them. A child needs a peaceful, safe environment, and I really didn't have that because the one who was supposed to protect me was hurting me.

I expected God to be like my earthly father. God had to demolish that mindset and change my beliefs, because I was scared to ask God for anything. I felt like I wasn't worthy, or I was a burden to him—or I haven't been good enough, so I didn't deserve to ask for my daily needs. I was afraid he would tell me no. When someone does that way too much, that's a form of rejection, especially when it's a need rather than a want (which there's nothing wrong with either).

When the devil would come charging at me like a bull, ready to plow right at me with his horns, I would go into a panic attack and wouldn't think God would be there to protect me. I would get so mad at myself, I would cry out to God, saying "I want to believe. I'm trying, but I can't—it's so hard!" God the Father understands the weakness and frailty of humans. He knows you're trying your very best, but victory doesn't come from anything you can do on your own. The Holy Spirit was showing me that I needed to make it my mission to build up my faith more than anything. I also needed to learn about love, because faith operates only in love.

But from that point on, when the Holy Spirit revealed to me that my real problem was doubt—doubt that He could protect me and keep me safe from harm," I was out to make it my priority to make my faith stronger. I also believe He said, "You can't rush your process, only hinder it." Think about that, because it will occur in God's perfect timing. Whenever those murderous thoughts crept up in my mind, I began to say out loud, "No, I love my husband, and I bless him, in Jesus' name." I would gird up the loins of my mind as tightly as I could so he wouldn't get me to that anxious point. I would speak the word out loud and pace back and forth, because I meant business.

But now that I'm mature in faith, I've learned another powerful weapon of warfare: singing to God. The enemy hates it with a passion when we do that because we are putting all our focus on God and not him. The enemy wants it all to be about him, and he wants people praising him. When I worship or sing unto God, I don't sing worldly songs to him but Christian worship songs that lift him up. When we start to do that, God's fighting for us. Several stories in the Bible document singing as warfare. Here's one verse that proves it: "After consulting the people, the king appointed singers to walk ahead of the army, singing to the Lord and praising him for his holy splendor. This is what they sang: "give thanks to the Lord; his faithful love endures forever!" I want you to go back and read that story. Why put a worship and praise team before the army? You will have to go back and read it to find out why.

When all this started, I was trying to do everything in my power to keep certain people around me to watch over me. But they couldn't help me, because I would still have anxiety attacks. God allowed the people to be removed from my life because He wanted me to run toward my giant, not away from him. So many of you out there right now have been running from your problems so you could get those horrible thoughts out of your mind. The devil will keep picking on you and will not leave you alone if he knows you're weak and not strong in your faith in Jesus. I can't promise you that once you are strong in your faith he will never come back to you ever again. However, if he does, you will be so strong in your faith and confident in God Almighty you'll show Satan you've got something for him. I've learned in your dark place, light has to shine; in your dry desert, it has to rain; in your rough spot, it has to get smooth; and in your valley, there is a mountain top waiting for you to climb.

Writing this book seven years later and looking back now, life is completely different. I say that because I've changed, even though Satan and his attacks might not have. But how strong God has made me, compared to back then. And I'm getting stronger and stronger each day in my faith and confidence in my God. I'm not perfect, but I know now when that spirit of fear comes, I take quick action and stand my ground. Not too long ago I would shrink back, say nothing, and try to ignore him, but I'm still learning to stand up, open my mouth, and fight. As I said, I'm not perfect, but the Lord's helping me to really get it down and face many fears that are uncomfortable for me.

Fear comes in many faces, such as fear of confrontation when things are not right. God has had me face people concerning my marriage and my personal life, going back to an environment I didn't think I would visit again. I've had to face people who were being fake or giving me dirty looks like, "Why are you here again"? I was able to smile and love them. I've faced authority trying to be crafty towards me; I've led a women's group; dealt with big financial decisions; I could go on and on, because even though fear has gripped me, by the leading of the Holy Spirit, I was able to do these things. We need to stop tolerating situations and people in our lives who pull us away from God, our peace of mind, our joy, and just daily life. We don't need drama distracting us, because Satan can try to work through anyone or anything to take us down.

Endnotes

1. 2 Chronicles 20:21 (NLT)

chapter 15

CLEANING HOUSE/KEEPING IT CLEAN

Before I wrap this up, I'm going to give you a list and a plan as your reminder and a navigator to your freedom. One thing I know is, faith requires daily action for it to be real faith, but I'm also here to reminding you not only how to get free, but stay in that position of freedom. I've heard people say all the good things about their freedom and liberty, but I always wonder, "What did you do? How long did you endure your trial? And most importantly, how do I keep on keeping on and not go back?" That's Satan's plan, to pull you right back where he had you, and I've seen it in some people's lives. It's sad, but only God can and will keep you from that because you trust in Him, and you know He's the only one who can help you.

I want you, with the Holy Spirit's help, to sit down with a pen and paper or your electronic device and map out your day, including spending time with God. Example: I would set my alarm at nine o clock, get cleaned and washed up, then go straight to my prayer room and spend at least an hour with God. During that time, I would soak in his presence, putting some soft and slow music onto help still my mind. Then, I would just wait to hear His voice, or anything he wants to show me. I would meditate on that, write it down, and thank him for showing me His heart. Then I would praise Him for who He is and how good he is to me, singing and praying.

I had to get really organized with my prayer time, because I was getting scattered brained and felt aimless and ineffective. I scheduled Mondays to pray for overseers of our church, pastors, and church staff, and I wrote down a couple of scriptures on each day to help me pray God's will, and it keeps me on track. Tuesdays, I pray for marriages and relationships, because that's more important than anything thing else besides our relationship with God. Wednesdays, I pray for services, saints (the church), and salvations. We all know to keep the church functioning properly and advance God's kingdom, we need to pray for these people. Thursdays, I pray for finances, jobs, and businesses, because it's warfare in these environments. We need to show our little world Jesus shining through us, and we need to be a good steward with God's money. We also need ideas to help us bring in more income to help others, not only ourselves. Fridays, I pray for destiny, anointing, and gifts. I like to pray for God to reveal to me ideas to minister to people. Also, we don't need to get big-headed about anything God gives us, or when he elevates us to amazing places we've never dreamed of.

Saturday is personal reflection day. This one is so crucial, because remember we don't want to get deceived, distracted, and destroyed by the enemy. We must look at ourselves and our motives with people. Are we loving and treating people right? Are we starting to get negative again when the money isn't rolling in, or because we're feeling sick? Am I on the right track with God, and do I need to practice more patience and quietness in my soaking time? Is there a hidden sin within, and maybe I'm not seeing it as I really should? Do I read my Bible daily? And am I staying out of people's business, focusing on my house and cleaning up some things?

Sundays, I pray for the nation, the city, and the state. I'm not going to lie but many times I have forgotten to pray for Israel. Thank God for the Holy Spirit, who is my reminder when I need one for things like that.

It's so important to pray for our nation and city, because the devil doesn't sleep, and we need to be the eyes and ears around us, praying the will of God, which is the word of God. Our prayers never are in vain when we pray and believe in our hearts, and we will see the change—it may not be quickly, but it will happen. We need to pray and bless our leaders whether we like them or not, because if we don't start praying the Bible over their lives, we could be in a living hell. When we don't speak up in our prayers for God, Satan has his own people who are sold out to him to do evil in our land, releasing curses and trying to harm people and our environment. We need to rise up, take our place, and do God's will. I know it isn't easy, but our eternal reward awaits us with God.

After that hour is done, I would get into my Bible. Always pray before you get in it and ask God to open your eyes and ears to see and hear him in his word, and then study it for a little bit. Start mapping out your week so you're not overwhelmed about the household things that need to get done. Like, on Monday do laundry, Tuesday clean your floors, Wednesday, write out your grocery list and dust, etc. It's just an example, but with God's help, you will figure it out. I know you're wondering what this has to do with the subject at hand. You need to get your house and life in order, because fear and anxiety can come from the details of everyday life. It all matters, and it all ties in together. God sees your daily routines, and routine is not a bad thing. We need to get our lives in order and stop weighing ourselves down with things that are robbing us from a blessed life.

Now I will take you through a quick preview into getting yourself and your life around you in order. First, pray the scriptures that you need over your life. Study your Bible—don't just zip through it. Find some resources to help teach you how to do that. Sing praises to God, because it gets your focus off yourself and your problems. It also means your battle is being fought in the spirit. Soak, quieting your soul and allowing the peace of God to saturate you on the inside. Let God download somethings into you, like his love. Who doesn't need God to tell them he loves them, or witty ideas that could help you out? He may have songs he wants to down load in you, or maybe he wants to warn you about something because he doesn't want to see you hurt.

The last one, which could be a challenge: worship him with every part of your being and with your everyday life. Stop hanging around people who gossip because you get an ugly feeling when that happens, and you feel something isn't right. It's the Holy Spirit warning you not to gossip, or to back off from that person. Keep your ears away from bad talk and music—listen to good things, because it will go down into your heart and show up in your life. Put your eyes to good and pure things that feed your soul. Stop putting your eyes to pornography or going to strip clubs and bars, because it will taint and stain your soul—do whatever you can to keep it clean. And go out and pray for people who are sick, busted, and disgusted so to speak.

Show Jesus by helping someone clean their house because they're busy working, and you know they don't have time. Pay for someone's meal; give out a word of encouragement; pray over your meal in public, because the world around us need to see there is a remnant of God's people in the world who honor and respect Him with all their heart, soul, mind, and strength. People need to see that, and who cares what they say or do? God is with you, and He has the final say. God is having me take back more ground in my life that the enemy has stolen. It's not always easy, but it's rewarding. I don't want you to think you will never feel any type of fear again, but as you give more areas of yourself to God, the enemy has no chance at taking things away from us ever again. The Holy Spirit told me, "Submission is gaining, not losing." That's a powerful but truthful statement. I want to encourage you, my brothers and sisters: keep fighting the good fight of faith, because it's a good fight. We need our faith.

DISOWNED TO ACCEPTED
sinner's prayer

If you want to know your heavenly Father through a relationship with Jesus Christ and desire to gain wisdom, knowledge, and understanding through his Holy Spirit, say this prayer out loud in humility and courage, with all your heart, and mean it.

Father God, in the name of Jesus, the name that is above all names: please forgive me of all my sins past, present, and future I believe my sin is now washed away with your blood, never ever to be remembered or brought back up again. Jesus, I believe you died and were raised from the grave three days later for me to rise up in victory. Jesus, I believe you're the son of God—be my Lord and savior. Jesus, baptize me with your Holy Spirit, with your holy fire and your perfect love, so it can start to over flow to people and make a difference in their lives and mine. In Jesus' name, amen.

GETTING THE DEVIL OUT OF YOUR DETAILS
deliverance prayer

Once again declare this out of your mouth with the authority Jesus has given you and believe with all your heart this breakthrough deliverance prayer.

God in Heaven, in Jesus' name, forgive those in my bloodline or family that have opened up the door of the demonic to sin of all kinds like fear, doubt, pride, and other things I may not know of, from the time of Adam and Eve up to now. And I choose this day to forgive them for everything they knowingly and unknowingly did here on earth that was passed down to me. I declare by the power that's been given to me in the name of Jesus, every curse, sinful habit, hang up and stronghold of the mind has been broken by the resurrection power of Christ. Lord. I declare you are closing all those doors in the spirit realm that were open.

Help me to close up those gaps and raise up those hedges here on earth by staying submitted to you all the days of my life. I declare all ties to Satan are cut off right here and right now, never to be passed on to me and my seed from here on out. Holy Spirit, the Bible says you are my teacher[1] and I ask you to teach me all things and please remind me everything you have said in the Bible. Remind me when the devil wants to bring up my past and my mistakes that I'm a new creation in Christ.

Teach me and remind me of the power and authority that's in your name (Jesus) when darkness wants to overtake me, and give me the courage to live out my new identity before all men fearlessly. Jesus, I choose today by faith to forgive every person who has personally wronged me or anyone I'm close to, past, present, and future. I know it's impossible to truly and completely forgive on my own, but you said you will not forgive me if I don't choose to forgive others as well. Open up your love to me so I can bless them, not curse them with my mouth. Thank you for a new fresh start and new beginnings. In Jesus' name, Amen!

Endnotes

1. John 14:26

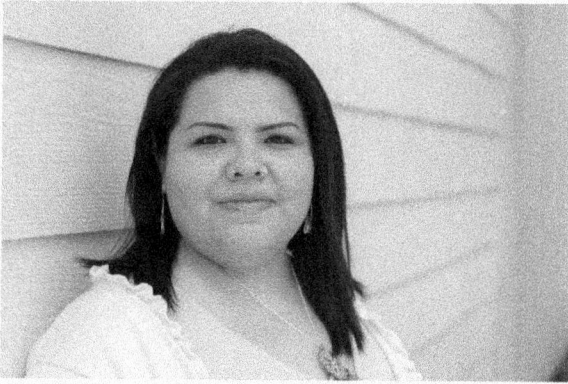

about the author

Cecile Vasquez is an author, encourager, wife and mother. When teaching, she likes to make things as simple as possible to allow the Holy Spirit to do the work in people's hearts. She has her own unique way of delivering the word and sharing very openly about her life's journey because she believes we can best relate to the world if we are willing to share our wounds.

Her journey has not been easy, but having people praying for and encouraging her made a huge difference along the way. More importantly, she became her own greatest cheerleader. Her favorite advice is to not only "get in the word, but let the word get in you."

Cecile is a wife to her loving husband, Mario, and mother of one little boy, Nehemiah, who is home in heaven with Jesus.

www.CecileVasquez.com

WORKS CITED

- *The Bible.* The English Standard Version. *Biblehub.com.* Biblehub,

- 2016. http://biblehub.com. Accessed 16 August 2017.

- *The Bible.* The Living Bible. *Biblehub.com.* Biblehub, 2016.

- http://biblehub.com. Accessed 16 August 2017.

- *The Bible.* The New Living Translation. *Biblehub.com.* Biblehub,

- 2016. http://biblehub.com. Accessed 16 August 2017.

- *The Bible.* New Heart English Bible. *Biblehub.com.* Biblehub, 2016.

- http://biblehub.com. Accessed 16 August 2017.

- *The Bible.* New International Version. *Biblehub.com.* Biblehub, 2016.

- http://biblehub.com. Accessed 16 August 2017.

- "Intervene." *Dictionary.com,* http://www.dictionary.com/browse/

- intervene?s=t. Accessed 16 August 2017.

- Mikeschair, "Someone Worth Dying For." *A Beautiful Life,* Curb Records, 2011.

All verses are taken from the New Living Translation of the Bible, unless otherwise noted.

www.ingramcontent.com/pod-product-compliance
Lightning Source LLC
Chambersburg PA
CBHW071149090426
42736CB00012B/2287